Saratoga Springs

A Memoir of the 40's and 50's

By Lewis M. Elia

Edited by Jacquelyn Wolf Birch

Trafford rev. 06/25/2019

 www.trafford.com

North America & international
toll-free: 1 888 232 4444 (USA & Canada)
fax: 812 355 4082

To my friend, Tom Bosley

Acknowledgments

The author would like to thank the following people for their help and support:

Mary Ann Fitzgerald, Historian for the City of Saratoga Springs and Ruth Ann Messick of Heritage Hunter for supporting this project.

Jamie Parillo, Director of the Saratoga Springs Historical Society and Curator, Erin Doane for their support.

John Conners, Researcher for the Saratoga Springs Historical Society for his work in locating the photographs from the George Bolster collection which are being used in this book.

My long departed friend Ray Calkins, native of Saratoga Springs and great artist whose love of our city and its beauty was such a factor in my life.

Writer and Humorist, Frank Sullivan who was such a good friend and who taught me so much about writing and life.

TABLE OF CONTENTS

PREFACE

The decades of the 40's and 50's were a transition period for the city of Saratoga Springs. The Golden Era of the grand hotels and gambling casinos was ending and it would take two decades for the city to enter a new period of growth. It was during this time that Saratoga Springs was really a small town. Only two things remained from the old days, the racetrack and the springs.

The springs, which fed the baths, brought in some people, mostly senior citizens who were, for the most part, not gamblers. The old Jewish hotels, some offering Kosher kitchens and some not, were slowly disappearing as their senior citizen population declined and the next generation opted for the resorts in the Catskills. When the racing season opened (Saratoga had twenty-one days of exclusive New York racing) the city was like an older woman who had sold off most of her assets but saved one good piece of jewelry which she wore out once a year. People would rent their houses to horse owners for the month and earn enough to pay their property taxes. Boys sold racing forms and tip sheets to earn money for school clothes. Men turned their cars into taxicabs and shuffled people from the Hotels to the track. When August ended and September arrived, the city turned into a small, upstate New York town as all the summer visitors went home.

Saratoga Springs began to change dramatically when the Saratoga Performing Arts Center opened and became the summer home of the New York City Ballet and the Philadelphia Orchestra. The new wealth of the country would now be in the hands of the corporate managers and the city's growth would reflect this. There was a big difference between the people who controlled the old money and the new money managers. The old money families had been like royalty. They came from a class of people who had been wealthy for generations. They were well educated and well traveled. Some spoke other languages and had traveled to the great European cities like Paris and Rome. When they returned, they built structures and monuments based upon their classical educations-The Italian Gardens with its beautiful statues in the Congress Park, the Yaddo Gardens, and the granite staircase in the park to mention only a few. Even the hotels reflected this exquisite taste. Noteworthy was the staircase in the Grand Union Hotel and the beautiful gardens and fountains in the United States Hotel. When these beautiful structures were finally torn down, the new American corporate culture would step in and build over the rubble. The elegance that was once Saratoga Springs would be gone forever.

Those of us who lived in the city during the 40s and 50s witnessed its decline and rebirth. During this transitional period, we lived in our small town. We walked down the main street and knew almost everyone who passed. We take with us the memories of that place which we will never see again. This book is a memoir of that time period: a time when most of the people we knew were born in Saratoga Springs and everyone liked drinking the mineral water.

Lewis M. Elia

March, 2004

THE GRAND UNION HOTEL

The Grand Union Hotel, circa 1950 just before it closed - photo by the author

The Grand Union Hotel, long a symbol of Saratoga Springs' prosperity and elegance was razed. Just before the wrecking crew got there in 1952, I took a walk on the Hotel's great front porch. The structure occupied an entire city block and the wide front porch extended the entire length of the block which fronted on Broadway between Washington and Congress Street. While I was walking down the length of the porch, I looked for the last time upon a floor made from beautiful white Vermont marble. This much marble would be worth a fortune today. I realized it would never be replaced. It was like taking the marble facing from the Roman Coliseum or the bronze from Hadrian's Pantheon. No one would ever build it again.

Eventually, I came to the middle of the block where the main entrance to the Hotel was located. I looked inside and saw the grand staircase, the Hotel's signature piece, once featured in the motion picture, *Saratoga* starring Clark Gable and Jean Harlow. (Another movie, *Saratoga Trunck,* was filmed at the United States Hotel and starred Gary Cooper and Ingred Bergman.) I would be seeing that staircase intact for the last time. Just before the Hotel was torn down, the owner of Quinn's Colonial Tavern, located just across the street from the Grand Union, purchased some of the staircase newels and made them into lamps. In this way, a small piece of Saratoga Springs history would be saved. Some years later, the Colonial Tavern burned down and unfortunately, they were lost.

I noticed all the store fronts which had been built to open to the street side were empty. I stared at them and thought about how they had looked during the Christmas season when the merchants decorated them with multicolored lights. I gazed into the empty windows and imagined the Christmas trees spreading their arms over toys no one could afford. The empty windows stared back, looking for several small boys and girls, all bundled up and shivering with the cold, peering into them to see the beautiful and colorful things the window had to offer. I walked on.

In a short time it was all gone. After the summer season of 1952, the building was demolished and a huge hole was cut in the fabric that was Saratoga Springs. The old hotel had covered an entire city block. The only thing left standing on that vast remaining space was a gray stone Episcopal Church which had occupied one lot on the Washington Avenue side. The Hotel had been built right around it. It was the first time in many years the Broadway side of that church had seen the light of day. It would be that way for a long time.

Eventually, a developer would buy the property and build a strip mall. Saratogians were appalled at the sight of a supermarket and Laundromat standing in place of the Hotel. Just after the strip mall was completed, I was sitting in The Colonial Tavern with my friend Ray Calkins. Ray was our local resident artist and a person who loved Saratoga Springs as much as he loved art.

"Just look at the building that replaced the Grand Union Hotel, Ray," I said.

Ray turned his head and looked out the window. "They must have gone to a cheese company to get the architect ," he commented.

Ray Calkins - Photo from the Saratoga
Springs History Museum

3

Photo from the Saratoga Springs History Museum

Ray's remark hit home with my group of friends as we gazed at the parking lot and cheese box-like buildings that stood where the beautiful old structure once took in the elite of the Saratoga summer crowd. Sitting with us was Frank Sullivan, a Saratoga Springs native and well known free lance writer for the New Yorker magazine. Frank was a man who was never at a loss for words. All he did was chuckle.

The Colonial Tavern was a favorite watering hole for Saratoga's elite and one of Frank Sullivan's favorite places. Many of Frank's celebrity friends came to visit him here. One I remember very well was the writer and playwright, Thorton Wilder. Many other celebrities visited the tavern as well. Among others I remember were crooner, Bing Crosby (who owned many horses) and member of the baseball hall of fame, Yogi Berra. It was also a nightly stop for our own local celebrity, motion picture star Monte Wooley who lived in Saratoga Springs.

Photo by the author - 2004

This is the site of the old Grand Union Hotel as it looks in 2004. The corner is Washington
Street and Broadway. The new complex is a mixture of retailing, office space and residential.

THE WORDEN INN

Photo from the Saratoga Springs History Museum

On the corner of Broadway and Division Street once stood the Worden Inn. The Worden was one of the smaller, elegant hotels in Saratoga Springs and was still operating in the 1950's. Although smaller than the Grand Union or United States Hotels, the Worden's porch gave the guests a view of Broadway traffic as good as any.

In the 1950's, the Worden was a throwback to the old horse and carriage days when service jobs, like bellhops were known, in the popular language of the day, as "colored men's jobs." As late as the early 1960's, all the bellhops in the Woden Inn were African-Americans. All other personnel, like desk clerks, bartenders and managers were white. One man in particular that I remember very well was "Alex" (I never knew his last name). He had been working as a bellhop in the Worden Inn since he was a kid. His Father came to Saratoga Springs as an exercise boy, got a job in the Worden as a bellhop which Alex took over when his father died. Alex retired when the Inn closed and changed into a motel.

My favorite Worden guests were the Spanish American War Veterans. Once a year, the group would hold its convention there and sit on the porch, rocking away the days reminiscing on the battles they fought in Cuba. The first time I saw them, probably about 1946, they numbered about thirty. Some were wearing paper hats and others were in full dress uniforms. Most were wearing their service decorations, proudly displaying the rewards they received for defending their country and the Monroe Doctrine. As the years passed, their group became smaller and smaller until only two vets, one highly decorated and in full dress uniform were the only ones remaining. The rumor began circulating that there was a bottle of expensive champagne that was to be opened by the last man. Finally, one year, no one showed up for the convention. Later, I read in the newspaper that they were both in a nursing home. I could never find out if there really was a bottle of champagne and if the last vet still had the strength to open it. The following year, the AP carried a story of the death of the last Spanish American War Veteran. And thus, the final chapter of the war that made Cuba independent of Spain and Puerto Rico a United States territory came to a close and their annual convention passed into Saratoga Springs history.

Photo by the author - 2004

In 2004, the Saratoga Downtowner Motel occupies this site. The site changed with the times as the parking lot was built where the porch once faced the street. The old Worden Inn, built in an era when everyone came to Saratoga Springs on the train had no provision for parking and could not survive in a world built around the automobile.

THE COMMUNITY THEATRE (ER)?

Photo from the Saratoga Springs History Museum

The small town of Saratoga Springs had two movie theaters. On the north end of Broadway's commercial district was the Community Theatre. On the south end near Congress Park was the Congress Theater. Both were owned by the same company.

The Community Theatre was THE upscale theater in town, that is , upscale for 40's and 50's Saratoga. Here was where all the main line motion pictures were shown. It featured comfortable cushioned seats and a red velvet curtain. The lobby had red rugs and beautiful black leather covered sofas. The ladies room was upstairs on the left as you entered the theater and the men's room was upstairs on the right. Great pains were taken to keep the restrooms clean. The facility showed the most current films, like academy award winner *From Here to Eternity* and films of that caliber.

It was also the only theater I ever knew with a railroad line running directly in back of it. It was quite an experience to have a loud freight train rumble through the back of the theater causing the building to shake in the middle of a performance. The motion picture industry would later spend millions developing new technologies which would cause a theater to shake during an earthquake scene. Saratogians were lucky enough to experience this long before it became fashionable.

An interesting sidelight is the spelling of the word theater. I never noticed the difference in the spelling until I examined these photos. The original builders used the Old English spelling. Whoever built the display cases didn't.

Photo by the author - 2004

The building as it looks in 2004 now serving office and retail space. Adaptive re-use replaced the marque windows. The ticket booth remains serving another purpose and the new owners solved the spelling problem by changing the name to "Community Building." Note the change in the landscaping.

Photo from the Saratoga Springs History Museum

On the south end of the Broadway business district was the Congress Theater. Here played the Saturday matinee which drew nearly every kid in town. Cowboy movies and serials were the main fare and here is where the popcorn was made for both theaters. Children's prices were available for those who were under twelve and Roy Rogers was "King of the Cowboys." If you were walking along Broadway in the middle of the afternoon, you might catch the strange sight of moving the freshly made popcorn from the Congress to the Community. The popcorn was made in the early afternoon and then brought up to the Community for sale at the evening performances. It was packed in large, brown cylindrical bags which, if stood on end, would probably be about three feet tall and about two feet in diameter.

A diminutive usher, with four of these bags tied to him with string, would walk up Broadway and deliver the popcorn to the Community Theater. Although the size of the bags made the load appear huge, the whole thing weighed about ten pounds.

Photo from the Saratoga Springs History Museum

Zooming in on the ticket booth one can clearly see that the theater opened at 2pm and the movie was shown continuously until 11pm, so you could pick your time (or stay all day.) On Saturday morning, the entire performance catered to kids and in addition to the standard fare of cowboy movies also featured serials. Kids could not wait to see the next episode of the serial which always had the hero in trouble when the episode ended. The hero, of course, always figured a way out in the next series.

My favorite serial was "King of the Rocket Men." Rocket Man had a bullet-like helmet and a rocket pack which strapped to his back and fastened in the front. It was a nifty piece of technology and beautifully simple to operate. The entire system consisted of two controls on his chest, a radio type button that could be turned to the "on" and "off" position and another labeled "up" and "down." NASA take notice.

ALL OF MY HEROES WERE COWBOYS

The following is an excerpt from *The Garlic in the Melting Pot,* by Lewis M. Elia and available on-line from Trafford Publishing, http://www.trafford.com/robots/02-0149.html. It has been edited for length.

Children all over America had many major influences that brought them out of their ethnic backgrounds and into the mainstream of American society. One was the great public school which helped them master the English language; mixing with people from other cultures. There was also the near-worship of sports heroes, mostly baseball players like Joe DiMaggio. All of these things infiltrated family life and contributed in various degrees to our upbringing, however, one of the most underrated influences on all American children was the impact of the American movie cowboy. In Saratoga Springs, the cowboy movies were delivered by the Congress Theater. Long lines of children could be seen on Saturday morning as children used their allowances so they could see their favorite cowboy heros.

The real American cowboy of the Old West was nothing like his counterpart movie cowboy made popular in the films produced in the 40's and 50's. The cowboy as a popular hero emerged in the years between 1865 and 1885 which saw the end of the Civil War and the expansion of the American west. A free and open spirit and a brand of rugged individualism, coupled with a lack of law enforcement authorities, which prevailed in the western territories of those days gave rise to the term "wild west." The real west and the west written about in the dime novels of the day were vastly different. Many of those stories were really romantic adventures aimed at selling the books to eastern couch potatoes who were eager for escape literature. Much of what was written, no matter how much the incidents they were based upon were true, rarely conformed to the actual facts.

History tells us the only true "gunfight" that ever took place was when Wild Bill Hickcock shot a man in the heart. Most gunfights were wild affairs and most men were really ambushed and shot in the back. Yet countless stories were told about gunfights between highly skilled warriors most of whom conformed to a code of honor and fought a fair fight..

Enter the movies, and the romance of the old wild west moved from the dime novel to the silver screen. Places like the Congress Theater could now provide a new technology that could provide a stage where the wild west could come alive to a mass audience. In typical Hollywood fashion, the old stories were re-written and new twists were added. Many more myths about the old west would grow from the movies. One of these had to do with the notion of wagon trains, attacked by bands of Indians. The settlers immediately drove their wagons into a circle, creating a fort as a way to defend themselves. In truth, settlers never did this. The first time it was ever mentioned was when it was depicted in an early western film made about 1933. Motion picture equipment was not very advanced in those days and a method of filming a wagon train under attack had to be found which would not require many movements of the camera equipment. The director came up with the idea to circle the wagons as a way to achieve this. So a technique invented for make filming easier exploded into an icon of the American west and "circle the wagons" became a phrase which to this day is still used to describe defending oneself.

The movie cowboy who evolved during the 1940's really reflected the ideals of the society at that time rather than any real person of the old west. The cowboy hero was always clean shaven and his clothing was always neat and clean. He was very chivalrous and never swore or used vulgar language. The considerable gun fighting skill he possessed was always used to fight the good fight, usually protecting the rights of ladies and hard working families from unscrupulous men who were trying to exploit them. He was unmarried, had a horse more intelligent and loyal than most of the characters in the film and he never seemed to have a job. He had no family of his own, answered to no one and always fought the honorable fight. He was fiercely independent, had a great singing voice and was as proficient with a guitar as he was with a six-gun. This hero always managed to win a fight even when he was framed, and always moved on after solving the town's problems and getting rid of all their bad guys. He always managed to pick up a "sidekick" whose antics provided the comic relief for the story line. He had all the attributes of a medieval knight with a handgun replacing the lance and sword.

To the 1940's kids, he was a saint. His success as a role model was so universal it crossed ethnic, social, economic and geographic lines. It made no difference who the kids were or where they lived, their heroes were cowboys. Irish, Italian and Jewish kids in Brooklyn attending the Radio Theater on Thirteenth Avenue in Borough Park every Saturday morning to worship these heroes just as Anglo-Saxon kids going to the Congress Theater on Broadway in Saratoga Springs did. Everyone owned at least a cowboy hat and a set of cap pistols complete with holsters emulating their favorite cowboy. In mock gunfights, we all wanted to be the good cowboy. We had to take turns at who was to be the bad guy and get shot. Sometimes we just got the guns shot out of our hands; other times we aped the actors and played out a long death scene. Bad guys always took a long time to die.

Children were greatly influenced by these cowboy images. A great deal of the morality of the time was taught through these films and their corny story lines. The biggest favorites were Roy Rogers and Gene Autry. They were quiet, unassuming men who could sing and fight. They had romantic interests but sex was not casual to them. They fought only as a last resort. They never started fights but always finished them. Their sidekicks were as famous as they were. Grouchy old Gabby Hayes in the Roy Rogers films and chubby Smiley Burnette in the Gene Autry movies were great favorites. Another favorite was Red Ryder. He described himself as a peaceable man but always managed to get pushed into a fight which he always won. He had a small Indian boy named "Little Beaver" as a sidekick. Little Beaver was actually a child actor named Robert Blake who later made motion pictures of his own and starred in a television drama as a New York City detective.

Great debates would take place as to who was the best cowboy. Some argued it had to be Roy Rogers because every film listed him as "The King of the Cowboys." Anyone could see his horse, Trigger was smarter than any other horse. Others claimed Gene Autry was actually better and his horse, Champion was as good as Trigger and did things which were just as smart. Since the majority of the opinions centered around Rogers and Autry, no one ever seemed willing to defend any other choice. If a brave soul actually preferred Red Ryder, he was reluctant to speak up for fear of being branded an idiot who knew nothing about cowboys. Since Roy Rogers was my favorite, I had nothing to worry about.

I don't actually know when it all ended. Like many things which change, it is difficult to identify the exact moment when cowboys fell from the pedestal and stopped being heroes. I think much of the blame goes to a new method of mass media which was about to burst upon the scene called television. The medium eventually made audiences more sophisticated and the next group of young people saw the old cowboy movies as pretty corny. Many years later my own children would ask me, "How could you believe any of that?" "How could they fire so many shots if they were only using six-shooters?" "If the Lone Ranger was really a Texas Ranger, who was his boss?" "How does he get paid?" "How come when people get shot, they never bleed?" These were good questions which never surfaced in my less sophisticated youth. Eventually, even I began to see the old cowboy movies as corny and my old heroes began to disappear. But they had already done their job. They made us all Americans.

A new kind of western, the adult western, would emerge. The central figure would retain some of the characteristics of the old cowboys, but now his clothing was dirty and less colorful and he was not necessarily clean shaven. His horse also lacked the colorful saddle and was no longer intelligent. His comic sidekick would vanish. New film technology would actually increase his gun fighting skills and people he shot would now bleed. He was still a loner, fighting the good fight, but sex was okay for him. Gambling, drinking and ladies of the evening suddenly appeared in the western towns. He could no longer sing. Eerie background music would replace the old western tunes. He was rarely killed, but was almost always wounded. Even African-American cowboys (there were many in the true old west) began to appear. The old cowboy was gone forever. The new cowboy liked women more than horses. Sorry old cowboys. I guess we just outgrew you.

And we outgrew the Congress Theater. TV could now bring the entertainment into the home and there was no need to go to the Saturday matinee to spend our allowances when all one had to do was turn the set on. The Congress Theater survived for a while as a roller-skating rink and a Chinese restaurant. It finally succumbed to adaptive re-use and now contains retail stores.

Photo by the author - 2004

In the spring of 2004, the space that once occupied the Congress Theater has been replaced by upscale retail stores reflecting the changes that TV and suburban malls had on the motion picture industry.

A ONE HORSE TOWN

The following is an excerpt from *The Garlic in the Melting Pot, Second Edition* by Lewis M. Elia.

One of the big events on West Circular Street in Saratoga Springs was the arrival of the thoroughbred horses a few days before the August racing meet began. One block up from my Grandmother's house was a railroad siding and open platform where the boxcars would stop to unload the horses. That site is now a senior citizen's center which now takes up what used to be the old Welsh and Grey Lumber Yard. The lumber yard used to use the siding for its deliveries as well. An historic sign now marks the area as "Railroad Run." Many years ago, the railroad moved the tracks far to the west side of town where they are now. There is an old freight house on the south side of the street which was converted to businesses and that's about all that remains of the railroad which used to thrive in the area.

West Siders loved to see the trains pull in with the horses. It meant mid-summer had arrived and everyone would be able to get some work. People could pay their property taxes by renting their houses for the month of August, taxis could pick up extra money ferrying people to and from the racetrack, my Grandmother could wash the jockey silks and take in August boarders. It meant my cousin Pat Ginocchi and I could sell tip sheets and pass out advertising for stars like Sophie Tucker and Joe E. Brown who were appearing at the Piping Rock Casino and other places. The small town of Saratoga Springs, with a population of about sixteen thousand, would come to life when about thirty to forty thousand visitors would arrive for the gambling and racing. It all started when the trains would bring in the horses.

The first time I remember the event, Dad took me there. We stood well in back of the loading platform next to the fence of the lumberyard as the trains pulled in, stopped and the boxcar doors were opened. Peering in, I could see the horses were standing in stalls, their rear ends facing us. The box car floors had been covered with straw and each horse had a teenage exercise boy traveling with it. The boys began leading the horses out one at a time, first backing them out of the stalls and then heading them out on the platform. A line of horses began to form and they were led out on to West Circular Street and began proceeding east toward the racetrack. I don't actually know how far the horses had traveled but my guess is they were being shipped up from New York City which had just closed it racing season. By law, Saratoga had an exclusive racing season in New York State which lasted something like twenty-one days, virtually the month of August. They had probably been traveling most of the day and, like any penned up animals, they did not take long to relieve themselves. All the way up the middle of West Circular Street.

"Dad," I said, "They're letting those horses poop all over the street."

"In this town, that's money," Dad mused, giving me my first lesson in economics.

As I think back on that scene today, I can't help but wonder how one attained the position of lead exercise boy. Obviously it was an enviable position to be in. Did they gamble for it? Was the position awarded on the basis of seniority? If so, was it the seniority of the exercise boy or of the horse? Was the value of the horse a factor? Traveling with horses in a boxcar and leading them down the street was already a tough job without having to be in the rear of that parade.

Adding to the drama of the event were the town dogs. Not many people owned automobiles in those days and traffic was very light on our street. Most neighborhood dogs were allowed to run loose. Once in a while, one would get territorial and show resentment for the intrusion of these animals into their domain and would begin barking at them, sometimes even chasing them. I saw one horse break loose and run into the empty lot on the north side of the street just past the lumber yard. It was bad enough being behind several of the other horses but these exercise boys really earned their keep when they had to chase down a powerful, frightened animal which had broken loose. The entire episode finally ended with the last person to come out of the boxcar, an adult pushing a little two-wheeled cart and carrying a broom and a scoop. His job, of course, was to sweep up after the horses.

Right after the horses crossed Broadway on to Circular Street on their way to the track, Dad and I walked downtown. We went into Liggett's Drug Store where Mr. DiSess, with his white apron and little paper hat was cleaning behind the food counter. Dad stopped to talk to Mr. DiSess and I began to wander around the store looking at various items which were for sale. There was a stack of post cards on a turntable rack. One caught my attention. It showed a man, pushing a two-wheeled cart, with a broom and a scoop cleaning up horse manure from the street. Under the picture was the caption, "Anyone who thinks this is a one-horse town should try sweeping up the streets in the morning!"

Photo from the Saratoga Springs History Museum

In the above photo, the photographer is looking west on West Circular Street just east of the corner of Union Street. The train platform is just behind the Welsh and Grey Lumber Yard and the empty lot where the horse ran when it broke loose is on the right.

This zoom in of the photo clearly shows the railroad crossing sign, the gates and the watch tower where the man who pumped the gates down for oncoming trains worked his shift. No photos of the unloading platform (in back of the lumber yard from this angle) could be located.

Photo by the author - 2004

The scene in 2004 shows several changes. The former grocery store on the left (the corner of Union Street) once owned by Joe and Marion Grasso is now a different type retail business. The old Welsh and Grey Lumber Yard has been replaced by a public housing project, on the right, not visible in the photograph.

Photo by the author - 2004

The railroad is gone and the section of Union Street on the right (approximately where the fire hydrant is now) was incorporated into the grounds of the housing project.

Photo from the Saratoga Springs History Museum

The building that housed Liggetts Drug Store burned down.

Photo by the author - 2004

This building replaced it.

Photo from the Saratoga Springs history Museum

One of many fires on Broadway which destroyed several downtown businesses. Pictured above is the fire that took place in 1957 which destroyed Liggets and several other buildings on Broadway's east side. The fire stopped at the Woolworth store which was constructed with a firewall. This kept the fire from spreading north.

KAYDEROSS PARK

The following is an excerpt from *The Garlic in the Melting Pot 2nd edition,* by Lewis M. Elia. It has been edited for length.

Everyone in Saratoga Springs loved Kaydeross Park. A short ride out to the lake would take you there. I remember seeing the lake from our car as we approached the steep hill looking down on the park and beach. Across the lake, about three miles away, I could see the familiar shape of Snake Hill, named because it looked like the head of a snake jutting out into the water. Our car reached the bottom of the hill and turned left toward the parking area and we drove along the bottom part of the road which ran parallel to the shoreline and the beach. The beach area was separated from the rest of the park by a chain link fence which ran all the way to the bath house. After changing in the bath house, we went through the footbath which was built into the ramp which lead to the beach where the rest of the family joined us. We staked out a spot on the sand and Mom put down a huge blanket. Once this was done, my cousin Pat and I would run and dive into the water of Saratoga Lake clean enough for swimming in those days. The swimming was good but no one could ever swim in the lake for very long and not cut a foot on one of the abundant fresh water clam shells which covered the bottom. After swimming, the next thing was to go to the steel gym set which sat back near the bath house and try various stunts on the trapeze, horizontal bar and rings for about a half hour or so until it was lunch time. We would get our hand stamped, leave the beach area and eat the lunch Mom had made. Dad would buy each of us a soda and give us a quarter so we could go to the penny arcade.

There was nothing like the penny arcade anywhere. Even Coney Island had nothing quite like it. This arcade had things which I had never seen anywhere else, probably because most of the items in it had been there since the 1920's when it opened. The best part was that in this B.C. era (before chips) everything really was a penny. The first great test of skill was to fire a chained down rifle which was resting in a rack. About twenty feet away was a bull's eye target. An electric wire ran from the rifle to the holding rack. When a customer put a penny in the slot and pushed down the lever, it activated the game. I activated it and aimed toward the black and white target. When I pulled the trigger, I heard a loud pop and a hole appeared next to the bull's eye. I could never get any closer than that but I always tried. The effects were done electrically with a beam of light hitting the target.

Next came the nickelodeons. They were mechanical movie machines. The customer could put a penny in the slot, turn the handle on the right and watch a two minute movie in living black and white! Once through the set of cards which made up the movie, the light inside the thing would shut off and would not go back on until another coin was deposited. There were about five different machines lined up in that section of the arcade and the titles were enough to entice any young boy into spending his pennies to see all of them. Shows like "The Artist's Model," "The Morning After the Night Before," "The Dance of the Seven Veils," (she only took off six veils) entertained just about every kid in Saratoga. The card sets had probably been there since the 1920's and featured dancers wearing tights up to their necks with long sleeves. The women would have rivaled any renaissance model for hip and breast size and were always facing the camera smiling.

Next came the inevitable test of strength. Two machines were featured. One was a miniature version of the carnival style strength test which had the operator swing a mallet at a lever which in turn sent a metal weight up a slide. Hit it hard enough and the metal weight would ring the bell at the top. Only teenagers and adults were strong enough to ring the bell but we tried anyway. It was a couple of years before my cousin Pat could ring the bell and another year after that before I could. We usually got it up to the point where it said, "Try again."

The next test of strength was Uncle Sam. He was a metal sculpture wearing a red, white and blue tuxedo with tails and displaying the stars and stripes on his top hat. He had a white, metal beard and stood there like a cigar store Indian, his blue, glass eyes staring blankly ahead, right arm extended, offering anyone in front of him a handshake. The fingers on his hand were fused together, pointing straight ahead except for the pinky which could move up and down. The idea was to grasp Uncle Sam's hand and attempt to close it by squeezing the pinky. Naturally, the pinky did not move until a penny was inserted in the slot in Uncle Sam's chest. Once that was done, the pinky could move but required more pressure as it was squeezed tighter. Anyone who successfully closed the hand was rewarded with a sign which would light up and display the words, "Uncle Sam Wants You." I guess Uncle Sam only wanted Pat and me together because it took both of us to close the hand and light up the sign. However, like the real Uncle Sam, he took our money anyway.

Next was a foolish little machine, about the size of a breadbox, sitting up on a metal stand. It had a glass front with lights and a metal grip in front. Put a penny in it, squeeze the grip and the lights would begin to go on, lighting up the scale displayed on the back. Wherever the lights stopped it would show how great a lover you were. It stopped at a different place each time so I guess lovers had their good and bad days. If it got to the top it would display, "World's Greatest Lover." If it didn't get to that level, the machine would place you in a slightly different category like, "Oh You Kid," or "You're Hot Tonight." Pat tried it and got, "Too Old to Cut the Mustard." Imagine, my cousin was only twelve years old and he was already past his prime. If that wasn't enough, I got, "World's Greatest Lover," which caused Pat to remark, "That machine doesn't work."

Then came Madam ZuZu who could see into your future. I had seen many such machines in Coney Island since just about every arcade had some version of a fortune telling machine, however, this one was much older than its Coney Island counterparts. I imagine the operators in Coney Island just kept scrapping them when they broke down but the owner of this arcade was able to keep his operating. Madam ZuZu was sitting in a glass case, and, judging by the wrinkles in her face, was the oldest person I had ever seen. She was wearing a peasant dress and was sporting a flowered bandana around her head. A deck of Tarot cards were permanently fastened to her left hand and she was staring down at four cards which she had already placed on the table in front of her. To the side of her cards was a crystal ball which I assumed no longer worked since she was relying on the cards. Placing a penny in the slot sent Madam ZuZu into action. First her head moved up, staring blankly ahead as if to get a look at the person who placed the penny in the slot. She always looked directly over our heads; we were too small to enter her line of vision. It must have been important to get a good look at the customer before she could read the future. Looking down at the cards again, she passed her right hand over them while moving her head from side to side. When her right hand finally came to rest, it pressed a metal lever releasing a little white cardboard rectangle which fell through a shoot leading out to the front of the machine. It must have required a great deal of energy on her part because the light in the case went out and Madam ZuZu returned to her original position. My fortune card said, "Good Things will be coming your way." Good job Madam ZuZu! Just what I wanted to hear. Pat's was even better. "You will marry and have children," it said. That turned out to be true. Too bad Madam ZuZu isn't still around. It turns out she really could tell the future and nullify the results of the love machine which told Pat he was too old to cut the mustard.

The final game was a lightbeam shooting machine gun (complete with sound effects) which was mounted and aimed at a movie screen about twenty feet away. A penny would send several World War I, bi-winged airplane projections across the screen with their engines screaming. It didn't take long to figure out there were only three places where they entered the screen and they always followed the same path. We learned to anticipate where the next airplane would appear and aimed the machine gun at it. If anyone hit a plane, it did not blow up; it only flickered and went out. The machine kept track of the score and another projection would post it next to the best score of the day.

After playing these games, we had a few cents left. These were usually spent on the Skee-Ball game. One cent purchased the use of three wooden balls which were rolled up a ramp into holes surrounded by wooden rings. The inner rings counted for more points than the outer rings and tickets were earned showing how many points were accumulated. It took a minimum of one hundred points in order to redeem a prize (off the bottom shelf only.) I got a Chinese Finger Torture which was a woven straw tube, open on both ends, where a finger could be inserted. Try to pull it out and the straw would grab it! The thing probably cost about two cents and I spent about fifty cents over several days to earn the one hundred points in tickets. The next shelf up had big stuffed animals which required one thousand points and the third shelf had a radio and a huge fancy glass bowl if anyone saved up ten thousand points. I never saw anyone take out a stuffed animal.

Eventually, the old machines just wore out and the management replaced them with the new electronic games which were bursting on the scene. Inflation changed the penny arcade into a nickel, then a dime and finally a quarter arcade even though the sign over the entrance still said "Penny Arcade." As the years went by, the arcade went the way of the merry-go-round and the park was sold to housing developers. The wonderful, honky-tonk world of Madam ZuZu and Uncle Sam would be pushed out of existence by sophisticated electronics But that's alright. They would have felt out of place in this brave new world anyway.

THE MERRY-GO-ROUND

The merry-go-round at the amusement park was a unique experience in itself. Because the park was a popular place for end-of-the-year school picnics, almost every kid in the surrounding area rode on it. Artistically carved horses gliding on brass poles would go around in circles for what seemed the longest time. The simulated horses were all painted in bright colors, mostly white with blue, red and gold saddles. The brass poles passed through each horse where the saddle horn would have been on a western saddle. Most of the horses were all carved in running positions, some with their heads down as if someone were pulling back on the reins catching the bit in the horse's teeth; others had their heads up as if they were finishing a jump. The ring of horses went up and down as the carrousel turned. If you were lucky, you could strap yourself into an outside horse and try to catch the brass ring for a free ride. Otherwise, you got stuck on the inside ring and had to wait until the next ride. You could also ride in one of the seats. This, of course, was only for adults since no self-respecting kid would ever pass up a ride on a horse to sit in a seat and just go around and around. What kind of fantasy would that have been?

One of the most fascinating things about the merry-go-round was the mechanical band which played during the ride. Crafted before the days of electronics, this marvelous thing would beat a bass and snare drum, clang symbols, toot a horn and play a piano with the precision of a real brass band. I counted at least six merry-go-round type songs before I heard one repeated.

As time passed, the little mechanical band began to break down. Although the tunes were still recognizable, some of the instruments no longer played. There must have been no one around who could fix it, because it was eventually replaced by an electronic tape recorder. Somehow, the tape recorder could never capture the sparkle of the little mechanical band which beat the drums and clanged the symbols. In time the Kaydeross Amusement Park was developed into condominiums. The merry-go-round was dismantled and the structure which housed it was renovated into an exercise club for the residents. The amusement park with its beautiful merry-go-round became a part of Saratoga Springs history.

Photo from the Saratoga Springs History Museum

Children on a picnic enjoying a ride on the Merry-Go-Round.

Photo from the Saratoga Springs History Museum

Children enjoying the other rides at Kaydeross Amusement Park.

Photo from the author's family album

This photo, taken in the late 1930's, shows the author's mother, Irene Scarano Elia (on the right) posing with a friend standing on the midway of the old Kaydeross Park. The old wooden bathhouse is visible in the background. The Penny Arcade, not visible in the picture, is on the left and the beach area is on the right. Mother had quite a battle with my Grandfather Scarano over wearing that bathing suit.

When the park was sold and converted to a housing development, the merry-go-round was dismantled and stored for many years. The city fathers decided to restore the ride and put it into Congress Park. Now, a whole new generation of children can enjoy it.

Photo by the author - 2004

Photo by the author - 2004

Artist and master craftsman, Lee Nicholls who helped with the original restoration of the horses does the annual touch-up as he readies the ride for the 2004 season.

Photo by the author - 2004

Kaydeross Park was developed into a condominium project. This view shows the area that was once occupied by the midway rides.

Photo from the Saratoga Springs History Museum

In the 40's and 50's, trains ran right through Saratoga Springs' West Side neighborhood. The above photo shows just how close one of the branch lines ran to the residential area. Many of Saratoga's immigrant population worked on the railroad and opted to live close to their work. Therefore, a good number of their houses were built close to rail yards that provided them with a living.

Photo from the Saratoga Springs History Museum

Looking south from West Circular Street, the main rail yards, the freight station on the left and the roundhouse on the right.

Many people wonder how people on the west side could live so close to the trains. I guess that if you were born and brought up in such a neighborhood, the trains became part of your life. I personally liked the old steam engines. They were like living, breathing animals. They would hiss, puff, and seem to be taking deep breaths as they reached back and pulled up all their energy. Sometimes a train would hook into a long line of freight cars with a bump. After the brakeman made the coupler secure, the engine would start forward and the sound of the tension it created on the coupled boxcar would snap in the air. As the tension pulled against each successive freight car, one could listen to the Doppler effect as each freight car responded.

Interview any of the residents who lived there at the time and one finds a sort of romance about the trains. This was especially true of the passenger cars. When the summer season began, the passenger trains would come in with the visitors. My favorite one was the train that arrived in the twilight of the early evening. Being near its destination (the passenger station was not very far from there) the train would be going slow enough so one could clearly see the passengers. The interior lights of the cars would be on and I could see the men and women, all dressed up, some holding their suitcases and bags ready to disembark and go into the grand hotels. Sometimes the dining car was clearly visible and there were still people sitting at the tables.

I liked to imagine who they were: entertainers, captains of industry, gamblers, tourists, and who knows what coming to Saratoga to see the racetrack open and take their chances. Sometimes a pretty woman would see us watching the train and give us a smile and a wave. We liked to think she was "Laura" in the song of the same name which said, "And you see Laura, on a train that is passing through..."

Photo by the author - 2004

The trains are now gone, moved outside of town. The street is not much different - the tracks are paved over and most of the old houses remain. The only thing missing is the romance that the train once brought to town.

Photo by the author - 2004

Looking south from West Circular Street. The tracks and roundhouse are gone and replaced by a tree-lined path called "Railroad Run."

THE A&P SUPERMARKET

Photo from the Saratoga Springs History Museum

This photo shows the building that housed "The Great Atlantic and Pacific Tea Company," which everyone knew as the A&P, a major national chain in those days. I remembered being able to walk through the store out into the alley in the back. Going through early in the morning one might see the deliveries being made down the back stairs. To make these deliveries easy, a wooden ramp with metal strips stretched from the alley down the staircase and onto the store's main floor. The employees slid boxes with various food items packed into them down the ramps. The ramp did not take up all the stair space so it was possible to walk up and down the stairs even when deliveries were being made. The best time to see this was when the fruits and vegetables were being delivered and their aroma filled the air.

My friend and classmate Tom Waring worked in the market when he was in high school and college in the 1950's. According to Tom, the most fun was the frozen chicken, packed in wooden crates with ice, which came down the chute rapidly and spun around when they reached the bottom. Tom had to make sure they were out of the way before the next box came down.

Between handling boxes and stacking food, Tom saw a lovely young lady named Claire Stanford who was also working there. It was like getting hit with a box of frozen chicken. At this writing they have been married for 45 years proving that even in the A&P true love can bloom.

As this zoom in points out, the supermarket prices have also changed with the automobiles.

Photo by the author - 2004

The building is still intact in 2004 with various retail stores replacing the market.

Photo by the author - 2004

A closer examination shows that the original building was once the YMCA.

Photo from the Saratoga Springs History Museum

Convention Hall was once the center of live entertainment for the city of Saratoga Springs. Many of the areas best athletes played basketball here when the hall was the site of the sectional basketball championships. In addition to the best high school players, it was also the home of the Saratoga Indians, a professional basketball team owned by prominent Saratoga businessman and civic leader, William Flannagan. If you were lucky, you could catch a game on a night when "Jock LaBelle," everyone's favorite referee, was in charge of the officiating and the refereeing was as entertaining as the game.

As I think back about all the things that happened here, one event stands out in my mind: a speech by Governor Thomas E. Dewey announcing the opening of the New York State Thruway. I don't remember much about what was said, mostly economic statistics and predictions, but I do remember Governor Dewey's final remarks. "Even the bums will have a place on the Thruway," reflecting the times when it was not politically incorrect to say "bums" rather than "homeless people."

Photo by the author - 2004

Convention Hall burned down in 1965. The site is now occupied by the YMCA building.

HATTIE'S CHICKEN SHACK

Photo from the Saratoga Springs History Museum

One of the most famous local restaurants in Saratoga Springs in the 40's and 50's was Hattie's Chicken Shack, owned by Hattie Austin Moseley, a remarkable woman, who came to Saratoga Springs in the 1930's as a seamstress. She opened her restaurant on Congress Street in 1938 and it quickly became a fixture in Saratoga's social life. I remember the checkerboard tablecloths, old wooden chairs and pictures of famous African-Americans hanging on the walls and the southern fried chicken and biscuits, which Hattie made famous in the area, and which no other restaurant could duplicate.

Many high school students made Hattie's their place to eat on Prom night and Hattie loved having them. She would come out of the kitchen just to see them dressed up in their gowns and dinner jackets and to talk to everyone.

Hattie also had a reputation as a street philanthropist, and the word was that she would help anyone who was truly needy. I never knew anyone who didn't like Hattie. She was one of the best loved people who ever lived in Saratoga Springs.

A zoom in of the picture shows Hattie standing in front of her door waiting for customers.

Photo by the author - 2004

Urban renewal took away the Congress Street location and Hattie eventually sold the business which relocated to Phila Street under the new management. The site that once contained Hattie's Chicken Shack is now the site of a shopping center.

Photo by the author - 2004

Hattie's new location is now on the corner of Phila Street and Lena Lane. Hattie passed away in 1998 and the restaurant, even under new management and offering a more extended menu, still offers some of Hattie's old favorites.

BARBER SHOPS

Before it became upscale, there were at least three barber shops within walking distance of the corner of Broadway and Division Street. The one I know the most about was owned by my uncle, Jerry Scarano and was located on Phila Street. It was on the left hand side of the street as one walked down the hill from Broadway. Actually, both my uncles worked there. My Uncle Jerry owned the shop and therefore worked the first chair while my uncle Frank Scarano worked the second chair and a fascinating character named "Tappie" Stone worked the third chair.

It was a time when men went to barber shops and women went to beauty parlors. Men's haircuts were short and women's hair was long. It was also a time when men might get a hot towel and a shave with their haircuts. I have some fond memories of my Uncle Jerry honing his razor on a strap getting ready to shave one of Saratoga's leading citizens.

During August there was always someone in front of the shop shining shoes. I even took a summer myself shining shoes for twenty-five cents a shine (fifty cents if you had brown and whites.) Thanks to my Uncle Jerry, my cousin Pat Ginocchi and I got that spot. The best place to be with a shoe shine stand was outside of a barber shop.

Uncle Jerry still had his shop at that location in the 1960's. I know this because like everyone in the world who froze that moment in time, he was cutting my hair when the news broke over the radio that President Kennedy had been shot

Photo Courtesy of the Scarano Family

In the photo, my Uncle, Jerry Scarano is turning on the barber pole getting ready to open his new barber shop.

Photo by the author - 2004

Today, the site of the old barber shop is now occupied by an art framing business.

There was another barbershop on Division Street located in one of the commercial spaces of the old Worden Inn. This one was owned by Frank Simone. Frank was in that location for many years and also served on as a school board member for the City School District of Saratoga Springs. He was a very civic minded individual and a very nice man. Over the years, Frank had numerous barbers who worked for him but the one I remember best was Joe Banjo. Joe, who lived on Saratoga Springs' west side, was a very personable man and excellent barber.

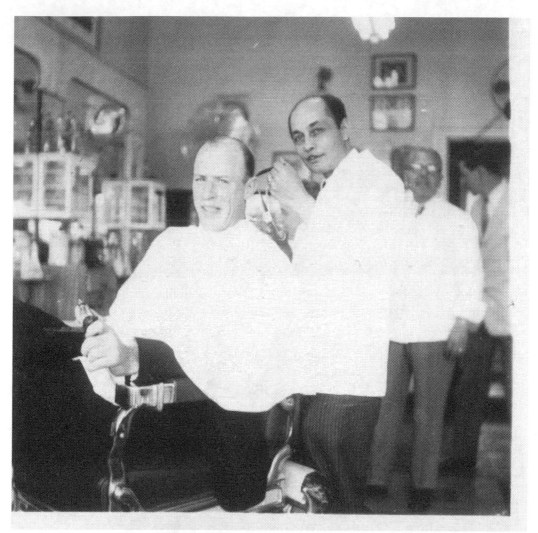

Photo from the author's family album circa 1955

Here is a photo I found in my family album showing Joe Banjo cutting Rev. Curley's hair. Father Curley was an assistant pastor at St. Peter's Parish. He spent many years studying in Rome and could speak Italian fluently. Needless to say he was a great favorite in the Italian community as well as everywhere else. When I asked my Grandmother Scarano how his Italian was, she said, "He speak-a very high class!"

THE CHILI BOWL

On Route Nine, south of Saratoga Springs, a local musician named Bernie Collins opened a restaurant called The Chili bowl. It featured a piano built right into the bar and many people spent their evenings there as Bernie played their favorite tunes.

The Chili Bowl had a chef whom everyone called "Softie." His claim to fame was a secret recipe for chili. Not being a chili afficionado myself, (I can take it or leave it) I could not tell you if the chili was really great or not. It seemed all right to me, but what did I know. Softie, however seemed to think it was the best chili ever made and he guarded the secret ingredients of the recipe like a sacred scroll. I remember many people asking him what he put in the chili and he promptly told them that he would never give that recipe away to anyone. I think many people were just prodding him about it for fun, but the more he was asked about it, the more he was convinced that everyone really wanted his formula. Rumor had it that he was so convinced of its value, he proposed marriage to a woman and told her he would give her the chili recipe if she married him.

♫... Isn't it romantic...♫

Photo from the author's family album

The sign went up on Route Nine announcing the opening of the Chili Bowl Restaurant. Notice the claim being made for Softie's chili: "Best Chili North of Texas."

Photo by the author - 2004

When Bernie Collins passed away, the restaurant was taken over by his son, Joe Collins who expanded the restaurant and featured his own name in place of the Chili Bowl. The expanded restaurant was much larger and offered a full menu. Joe Collins also passed away and the restaurant was sold and is now under a new name and management.

THE WALDRON MANSION

Photo from the Saratoga Springs History Museum

The Walworth Mansion was build in 1815 by Judge Henry Walton. Originally known as the Pine Grove, it was sold in 1823 to Chancellor Reuben Hyde Walworth. It was remolded and expanded in 1885 and served as a hotel for the Walworth family until 1912. It remained the home of the Walworth family until 1952. It then fell into a state of disrepair and was demolished in 1955.

The Saratoga Springs History Museum has preserved most of the furnishings and have them displayed on the third floor of the History Museum (The Casino in Congress Park.)

When I was in elementary school, my teacher took us by the Mansion and said it once served as a station for the underground railroad for fugitive slaves being smuggled into Canada. Although many places in the area did serve as stations for the underground railroad, I cannot find any documentation that the Mansion was actually used for this purpose.

Photo by the author - 2004

The site that once contained the Walworth Mansion is a gas station in 2004. Just to the left, not shown in the photo, is the Community Building. To the right of the photo is the old firehouse, now a restaurant.

Photo by the author - 2004

Photo by the author - 2004

The furniture from the Walworth Mansion was donated to the Saratoga Springs History Museum. The Museum used the third floor of the Casino building in Congress Park to put together the Walworth Museum Exhibit. There are more rooms on display than are pictured here.

Photo from the Saratoga Springs History Museum

In its heyday, the Saratoga Springs Train Station occupied a good part of the corner of Church Street and Railroad Place. Passenger trains would come from New York City and disembark passengers arriving for the racing season in August. Horse carriages would wait to take the visitors to the grand hotels, until the automobile arrived on the scene. In the 40's and 50's, taxi cab drivers would line up where the horses once waited trying to pick up fares.

Zooming in on the Railroad Place side of the train station, a diner and a newsroom becomes visible.

Zooming in closer, reveals the sign "Crawley Restaurant" which featured lunch, regular dinner and home cooking.

      Zooming in looking north toward Church Street we see the old coal yards owned by the Delaware and Hudson Railroad. This was a convenient location to store coal which was used by the steam engines. When the more efficient and modern diesels burst upon the scene in the early 1950's and the days of steam were numbered, the coal yards were sold to a private contractor who held them for a few years. Eventually, they were torn down

Photo from the Saratoga Springs History Museum

Also on Railroad Place opposite the train station was the Bullis Diner and Bullis Garage, owned by Simeon DeWitt Bullis and his brother-in-law, Wilbur C. Cowles. With his brother, W.W. Bullis, an attorney in Lake George, Mr. Bullis also owned, trained and drove harness horses. Mr. Bullis died at the age of 58 from complications resulting from a harness racing accident. Simeon's daughter, Simone Bullis Spaulding was my classmate in high school and has fond memories of her uncle and adoptive father, Wilbur C. Cowles, taking her to the Commercial Diner (just up the street on the left as you look at the photograph) early on Sunday morning when she was quite young. She recalls happily spending those Sunday mornings "helping out" at the garage. The Commercial Diner is shown in the next section of this publication.

Photo courtesy of the Bullis Family

The above photograph shows Simeon DeWitt Bullis holding his daughter, Simone, circa 1937. Mr. Bullis was known to help out many people who frequented the diner by lending them money, allowing them to use everything from wrist watches to stock certificates as collateral. Simone still has some of the items that people never returned to claim.

Photo by the author - 2004

The white building with the grey roof in the left background is a supermarket which was built on the old train station site. One of the few buildings left in the photo is the Saratoga County office building which used to be the old dress factory on the right. All other buildings that previously housed various businesses on Railroad Place have been razed.

Photo by the author - 2004

Railroad Place side of the old train station. Several new buildings have replaced the diners, newsrooms and auto shop that once thrived here. The old dress factory, converted to an office building, is the only structure that remains.

A zoom in shows the site of the old coal yards, partially blocked by the supermarket, which is now a city park and parking lot.

Photo from the Saratoga Springs History Museum

The Colonial Beacon Oil Company once stood on the corner of Church Street and Railroad Place. The unusual lighthouse tower was a landmark fixture in Saratoga Springs. Although not visible in a black and white photo, the trim on the tower and building was painted a bright orange. This photo actually dates to the 1930's but the scene was similar in the 1940's.

Zooming in on the photo yielded some interesting results. The commercial diner which advertised, "quality foods."

In back of the Commercial Diner is a building that was once a dress factory. That building is still intact in 2004 and contains some of the Saratoga county offices.

Photo by the author - 2004

In 2004, the site is occupied by a Stewart's gas station and convenience store. The lighthouse that was once a Saratoga Springs landmark is gone along with the Commercial Diner. The old dress factory is still visible in the background but has been renovated and now contains some of the Saratoga County offices.

SAINT PETER'S CHURCH

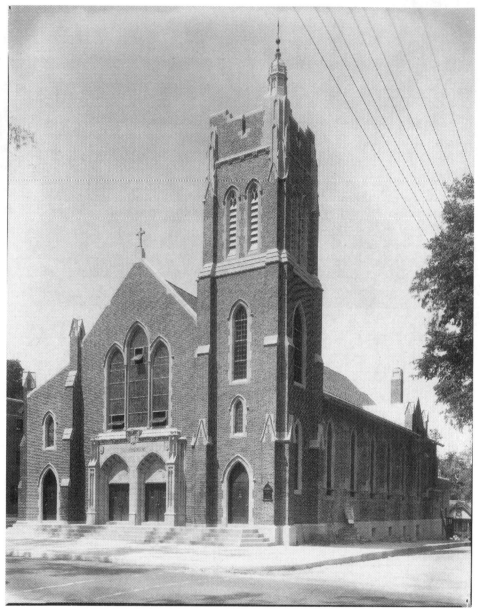

Photo from the Saratoga Springs History Museum

Saint Peter's Church is located on the south end of the Broadway business district. It was founded in 1834. It was the first Roman Catholic church in the city and later, when another church was opened on the east side of town, was the mainstay of Roman Catholics who lived on Saratoga Springs' west side.

Photo by the author - 2004

In 2004, the structure looks basically the same. The church was completely renovated in 1980 and now reflects the new philosophy that emerged out of Vatican II. Notice the front doors are sealed. Parishioners now enter from the side of the building.

Photo from the Saratoga Springs History Museum

Even in black and white, this old photo shows the beautiful interior of St. Peter's Church. It glows with stained glass windows, magnificent statuary, arches and columns.

Photo by the author - 2004

Also as part of the 1980 renovation, the interior today shows that the alter and the stained glass windows have been moved to the north wall on the right of the photograph. The pews have been removed in favor of new seating and the columns and arches have been replaced.

It had been many years since I had seen the interior of the church and the first time I saw the completed renovation interior was at a funeral mass. Having made my Conformation in this church, I was shocked when I saw the extent of the changes. When the mass ended, I asked one of the old Saratogians who was in attendance what he thought of the new look. "It looks like a ski lodge," was his answer.

I am not taking sides on Vatican II or the renovation. Beauty is in the eye of the beholder.

So what happened to the pews from Saint Peter's Church? They were purchased by the owner of the Old Bryan Inn restaurant. One can always tell when a parishioner comes to the restaurant by the look of guilt on his/her face for sitting in the pews enjoying themselves where once they made their First Holy Communion.

Photo by the author - 2004

Here is a shot of the author's wife, Linda and our friends, Carol and John Zanetti having lunch at the Old Bryan Inn in St. Peter's pews.

HOUSE ON WEST CIRCULAR AND HAMILTON

Photo by the author - 2004

The house on the corner of West Circular and Hamilton Street is virtually unchanged from the way it was in the 1940's. In those days it was owned by two older women, the Brownell sisters. One of my fondest memories of them was on Halloween. They always made caramel covered popcorn balls to give to the trick or treaters. It was not unusual to see twenty or thirty costumed kids lining up in front of this house trying to get one of the popcorn balls.

This house always reminds me that this was a time when even seven and eight-year-old kids could roam worry free throughout the city at night without having their parents with them. It was a time when two elderly women could open their doors to kids without the fear of being robbed. And it was also a time when kids could actually eat all the treats they collected without having to examine them for razor blades or pins.

I will never forget those two ladies who were so kind to the kids on Halloween.

THE AVENUE OF THE PINES

Photo from the Saratoga Springs History Museum

The Avenue of the Pines was constructed as an entrance to the Saratoga Spa State Park, a WPA project in the height of the great depression. It was a measured mile, exactly one mile long without curves. The photo above was probably taken in the early 1940's when the trees were not yet at their full height.

The road began at a traffic circle located near the bottling plant and ended at North Broadway. The North Broadway side intersected with Fenlon Street and formed a three-point intersection.

The Avenue was always closed during the winter months. Early in November, just before the first snowfall, a barrier would be placed on both ends of the road with a huge sign placed on it that read , "CLOSED FOR THE WINTER."

Sometime about the end of April, just after the snow plowing season ended, the sign and barrier would be removed and the Avenue would once again be open for traffic. This was always the way that old Saratogians knew it was spring.

Photo by the author - 2004

The Avenue of the Pines in 2004. The pine trees are approximately seventy years older then they were in the first photograph and the general setting remains the same. The road is now open all year leaving Saratogians to figure out when spring arrives on their own.

Photo by the author - 2004

This is the intersection of Fenlon Street and Broadway. The old Avenue of the Pines used to begin at this point. Because it intersected Broadway and Fenlon Street in a three point intersection, it was deemed too dangerous. In order for the road to make a perpendicular entrance to Broadway, a curve was built into it and the new entrance was brought about two hundred yards south of Fenlon, to the left as you view this photograph.

JERRY THE FRUIT MAN

On the corner of Division and Maple Streets there once stood a gas station and an oyster house. The gas station was demolished in the 1930's and the lot were the oyster house stood was purchased by a Mr. Jerry Guerriero, an Italian immigrant from Frigento, Italy. He came to America and served in the American Army during World War I. He brought with him a great deal of expertise on fruits and vegetables. The photo of the oyster house shown below which was taken in the 1930's is the only one we could locate in the history files.

Photo from the Saratoga Springs History Museum

Jerry began an open air fruit and vegetable market on that corner. He turned the old Oyster House into a fruit stand. It was built in the style of a pavilion, such as one could find in a park catering to picnickers, but with doors that could be closed and locked. Inside were wooden stands which contained open boxes and cases of fresh fruits and vegetables like none sold anywhere else. The unopened boxes were stored under the stands until ready to be sold and weighed on scales hung from the rafters. Jerry purchased most of the produce from Henning's farm just east of the city (where BOCES is now located) which assured his customers of the freshest fruit and vegetables available.

Many celebrities purchased the produce from Jerry, including singer, Sophie Tucker and movie star, Celest Holm. Jerry, unaware of the celebrity status of Miss Holm, was asked, "Do you know Celest Holm?"

"No, is it-a for sale?" he responded.

Jerry's daughter Rita and her husband Al Parisi sometimes worked at the store. Whenever Jerry left one of them in charge, he instructed them to keep the doors open, even when it was cold outside, which kept the vegetables crisp. Once he left, they would close the doors in an attempt to keep warm but Jerry would come back around the corner and always catch them.

Typical of an Italian man, Jerry was also known to help out people who were in need if there were children involved. Many people who were down and out would get credit from Jerry, simply because he felt sorry for their children. He just couldn't see them go hungry. Some never paid their bill. If a pregnant woman came into the store, Jerry would give her a free piece of fruit. "Thats-a for the baby," he would say.

In this sense, Jerry was like many of the small shop owners who gave such a personal touch to their customers, like Hattie Moseley (Hattie's Chicken Shack) and Simeon Bullis (Bullis Diner and Auto Sales). All were known to help people who were down and out. Imagine anyone going into one of today's corporate stores like Wal-Mart or Home Depot and borrowing $5 on their wristwatch!

One day, Jerry decided to have a new roof put on the structure. He instructed the roofing contractor to use different color tiles and spell out his name as follows:

JERRY THE FRUIT MAN

The man complied with Jerry's wishes but decided to play a small joke and added a single letter to the sign that Jerry did not order. The finished sign on the roof read:

JERRY THE FRUIT$_Y$ MAN

Jerry was very upset when he saw the sign.

"Whatsa this?" he bellowed. "I'm-a Jerry the Fruit-a Man not Jerry the Fruit-y Man."

He told the contractor that if he expected to get paid he would have to fix it. The contractor promptly climbed back up on the roof and painted the letter "y" out.

Jerry Guerriero
Photo courtesy of the Guerriero family

Photo by the author - 2004

In 2004, the location became far too valuable for anything like a fruit stand. The site is now occupied by a federal credit union. All the buildings on the commercial end of Division street from Railroad Place to Broadway have been razed and replaced with more modern structures. We would never see the wonderful world of "Jerry the Fruit-a Man" again.

THE SARATOGA PERFORMING ARTS CENTER

Photo by the author - 2004

The following is an excerpt from *The Garlic in the Melting Pot*, by Lewis M. Elia. It has been edited for length.

During the early sixties, I earning my living as a teacher in the Schenectady, NY City School District and spent my summers working as a life guard at the Saratoga Springs State Park. I loved my summer job. It was a teacher's dream come true. After being a life guard for many years, I finally became manager of the Victoria Pool (it was called the Gideon Pool in those days.) The manager's pay was better and I met many fascinating people, some of them famous, who were in Saratoga Springs on business and/or pleasure.

Swimming had always been my particular pleasure and I got to swim every morning before we opened to the public. I made a very good friend in the then Commissioner of Conservation, Dr. Harold Wilm, also a swimmer. He came to the pool with his wife whenever he was in town in order to relax and swim laps.

The Commissioner was a wonderful man. He was a quiet, unassuming intellectual who supported the arts. Dr. Wilm was one of the prime movers in getting the Saratoga Performing Arts Center built in Saratoga Springs and was influential in obtaining the support of Governor Nelson Rockerfeller and the New York State Legislature to grant money for the project. Dr. Wilm also addressed many Saratogians about raising money to support the center since the State only provided a small fraction of what was needed. It was early during the time of these negotiations when Dr. Wilm took a break and came swimming. We were talking about the management of the pool when he invited me to have lunch with him at the pool cafeteria.

"Dr. Wilm, I wanted to congratulate you on getting the state to provide the money for the SPAC project," I said. " I know how hard you worked on it and I'm sure it wasn't easy. I want you to know your efforts are appreciated."

"Thank you Lewis, " he responded. "Do you really think it will be good for Saratoga?"

"Of course," I said. "It will attract a nice class of people who appreciate the performing arts. Many will be wealthy and that will not hurt the town. We will finally have something here which will not be just in the month of August and it will give the people in the region a chance to be exposed to cultural activities now only available in larger cities. I think it's marvelous and I know it probably would not have happened if it weren't for you."

"Did you know I am getting a lot of opposition from the locals?" he said.

"No, I didn't. But let me tell you this. If you search history you will notice that every man of vision was opposed in his time. Socraties, Copernicus, Galileo to name a few. I'd say you were in good company. And let me add this: people remember Socraties, Copernicus and Galileo. How many people can name one of their detractors?" I offered. "The time will come when people will mention your name in connection with this project. Your detractors will not only be forgotten but (if any are still around) none will ever come forward and identify themselves." I said.

It was like a light went on in the Commissioner's eyes. I could see the faint traces of a smile on his face as he was listening to me. He interrupted his wife, who was sitting on the grass reading a book, and called her over to the table. He made me repeat what I said.

"Oh thank you so much Lewis," she said. "This is just what Harold needed to hear. It's been so difficult on him and he sometimes loses faith. This project is taking a lot of his personal time and energy and he finds it difficult to deal with the detractors. You have no idea how much your words meant to him. Thank you again," she said.

The thought crossed my mind as to how human Dr. Wilm was. Here was a well known man, a personal friend of Governor Nelson Rockerfeller, who was head of the New York State Department of Conservation. Thousands of people worked for him. He made speeches to countless organizations, universities and foundations. He was brilliant and respected throughout the country and yet human enough to feel the pain of local criticism and appreciate a kind word from a school teacher working on a summer job.

As the years went by, the Saratoga Performing Arts Center not only became a huge commercial success but people came from all over to see the New York City Ballet and the Philadelphia Orchestra perform in their new summer home. But neither the Commissioner nor I could have foreseen the impact the Center would have on the community. It became the turning point for an economic revival in Saratoga Springs which no one could have possibly predicted. The name of Dr. Harold Wilm will always be mentioned in connection with SPAC. I can't remember the name of a single detractor.

This picture, taken in the late 1950's, shows the author when he was a lifeguard and pool manager at the Victoria Pool.

THE SHOE SHINE BOYS

During the 40's and 50's, shoe shine stands could be found all along Broadway. It was a time when men took pride in their personal appearance, and having one's shoes shined was a critical part of that preen. There were no Michael Jordan or Nikes, leisure suits or cut-offs. Dudes would spend the money to have their shoes shined and their pants pressed because they wanted to look good.

Several teen-aged boys made a pretty good living during the summer months helping men achieve that goal. One such boy was my friend and high school classmate Robert Blais. Bob is a native Saratogian who has been the Mayor of Lake George Village for the past 34 years. He resided at 242 Nelson Avenue on Saratoga's East Side and was a star athlete at Saratoga Springs High School, graduating in 1954. His father and mother were members of the Brown Family who owned Brown's Beach on Saratoga Lake.

Bob has accepted my invitation to pass on his experience as a Broadway shoe shine boy and is contributing the following story to this publication.

SHINE 'EM UP

"Shine 'em up," was the cry heard from the attendants of at least three shoe shine stands which were situated on Broadway during the 1950's, trying to entice the many high roller gamblers that came into Saratoga Springs.

There were three stands operating on Broadway when I was working the summer trade. One was on the west side in front of Crompton's Restaurant. The other two were on the East Side, one in front of the old Palace Recreation Hall, and mine in front of Savard Brothers' clothing store. The Savard Brothers were very good to me. My "rent" for the spot in front of their store consisted of sweeping the sidewalk every day, lifting the awning up and down, and shining the Savard brother's shoes.

The stands were simply constructed and consisted of wooden platforms with a compartment for the storage of tools and supplies, topped with nailed down metal patio chairs. The shoe stands, where the customer placed his foot while sitting in the chairs, were made of iron and perfectly indented to hold the shoe in place while it received the shine. Prices ranged from twenty-five to fifty cents for most shoes, and up to one dollar and twenty-five cents for a two-tone. Two-tones were the favorite of the sportier customers and consisted of either brown or black leather rears and sides with a white front and matching brown or black toe. All shoe-shine boys were smart enough not to do the two-tones directly on the feet as it would tie up too much of the chair time. These had to be delivered to the stand and the boys would do them during the day when business was a little slower. A customer could pick up the spiffy two-tones at the end of the day just in time to start the circuit of Saratoga's night life, dinner, drinking and gambling.

Shining shoes properly was a real art. Applying the right amount of shoe cleaner with the brush came first, then two coats of polish with the right amount of "snapping the rag" to draw attention. As a finishing touch, most boys used a black liquid to "paint" the outside soles of the shoes to get a finished look and increase the chance of getting a tip.

Many prominent Saratogians like attorneys Lawrence Labelle and Leroy Walbridge were regular customers along with Judge Harold Amyot. In addition to these locals, I also shined the shoes of many celebrities, among which were Henny Youngman, George Raft, Dom DiMaggio and the famous Hall of Fame jockey, Eddie Arcaro. Also included in my regular clientele were many members of the Whitney family.

Many customers found that the shoe shine boys were a fountainhead of information and I personally sent many folks to Andy Desidoro's Ash Grove Inn Restaurant for dinner as well as the Colonial Tavern and Paramount Pete's. Many wanted to be directed to Congress Street and Hattie's Chicken Shack, a popular destination.

I also got paid to pass out "pink tip sheets" after I closed the stand for the day. These were self styled handicappers who would sell their tips to customers before the track opened. In order to convince the racing fans that they were truly good handicappers, they would get the race results after the sixth race, pick favorites for the remaining three and print up the tip sheets just in time to hand out to the fans on Broadway after they had left the track for the day. They were printed on pink paper (mimicking the daily racing form so that they would look official) and would proudly announce that they had picked several winners that day. The next day they would sell their tip sheets on that day's races hoping that some fans would remember they had picked six winners the previous day. They even had yesterday's "pink tip sheet" to prove it!

It was a long day. When it ended I was dead tired and I would ride my bicycle down Caroline Street on my way home to Nelson Avenue. I remember passing Bud Brophy's "Inn," the Turf, and Sperry's, some of Saratoga's most popular watering holes and the newsroom on the corner of Putnam and Caroline Streets that was booking bets. Then I would pass many of the rooming houses with folks in rocking chairs blocking the sidewalks.

It was a long day and hard work for a teen-aged boy. I learned a lot about being in business for myself. Later, I took these values with me into the business world and if I am successful at it today, I can attribute a great deal of it to the days when I hustled out on Broadway in the Saratoga Springs summer shouting, "Shine 'em up!"

Author's note:
Bob Blaise runs several successful businesses since he moved to the Village of Lake George shortly after he graduated from college. This is in addition to being one of the longest tenured mayors of any American city.

Photo from the Saratoga Springs History Museum

Savard Brothers, Inc. clothing store as it appeared in the early 1940's. This view is of the corner of Caroline Street and Broadway looking east. Bud Brophy's Inn is located in the basement under the store. The building is virtually unchanged today with other business now located there.

Photo from the Saratoga Springs History Museum

The United States Hotel was situated on the corner of Division Street and Broadway. It was the second largest hotel next to the Grand Union. This imposing structure was the scene of the motion picture, *Saratoga Trunk* starring Gary Cooper and Ingrid Bergman. The motion picture is still available on VHS and many beautiful shots of the hotel (which is called the Saratoga Springs Hotel in the movie story) appear in the film.

Zooming in on the corner shows the bar and tap room, a great favorite with the summer visitors as well as a barber shop. Notice the lady in the forground with the fashionable hat and the men on the upper porch on the Division Street side with their straw hats.

Another zoom in on the photo shows the elegant front stairway of the hotel which opened up on Broadway. Many guests liked to sit on the spacious front porch and read the racing forms before going for a day at the track. The staircase and the front porch were also the location set for many of the scenes in the motion picture, *Saratoga Trunk.*

Photo from the Saratoga Springs History Museum

The back of the United States Hotel featured a beautiful enclosed courtyard and garden with a spectacular planter as its centerpiece. There were also water fountains not visible in this photo.

The planter in the center was arranged to look like a fountain.

Photo from the Saratoga Springs History Museum

Shortly after the Hotel closed for good, the courtyard deteriorated badly. The loss of gambling and the fact that the Hotel could never accommodate the parking needs of the public now arriving by automobile contributed to the failure. The heyday of the Grand Hotel was over.

Photo by the author - circa 1954

The United States Hotel was demolished in the 1940's, the first of the large hotels to go. This photo was taken from Railroad Place (the back of the hotel) looking toward Broadway and was all that remained of the beautiful Victorian garden that once stood here. What was once one of the most beautiful gardens in the country was reduced to a sand lot.

The Division Street side of the Worden Inn is visible on the left. The building in the center was a supermarket.

Several buildings appeared on the Broadway side of the lot. For a short time the space was occupied by a deco style, cinder block building named *"The U.S. Bar"* which flourished for a few years. Subsequently, the bar was sold to a fast food chain restaurant called *"The Red*

Barn. " Believe it or not, the building was actually built to resemble a barn. I remember the city fathers at the time being happy to get anything that did business into Saratoga.

Older Saratogians, however, found it difficult to look at such a building on the main street along with the empty lots, because they remembered the elegant structure and beautiful gardens that used to occupy the site. Many remarked that Saratoga Springs had hit bottom. It would be that way for many years.

Photo by the author - 2004

The corner of Broadway and Division Street as it appears in 2004. A bookstore now occupies the corner and several other businesses now line Division Street. The only place that one can see what the United States Hotel was really like is in the film, *Saratoga Truck,* which also has some fine shots of the old train station and the springs in Congress Park.

EPILOG

I got the idea for writing this book on a recent visit to Saratoga Springs. Like anyone who visits his home town after being away, I couldn't help but see how much the small town I grew up in had changed. The Saratoga of the 1940's and 50's was quite different from the Saratoga of today. Old Saratogians must be mind boggled at the changes. I know I can't stroll around town without feeling it.

I thought about the places I had seen and the people who used to populate the city. I decided that some of my memories should be preserved for the next generations of Saratogians who would never get to experience what it was like. I decided to supplement the old photos from the History Museum with some of the memories I have of the people who lived here
.

When I began photographing the sites as they are today, a kind of sadness came over me. I felt I was writing the Saratoga version of *Gone With the Wind*. So many people and places have vanished. I hope I was able to preserve just a little bit of it.

It really hit me hard when I saw the bookstore now standing where the United States Hotel used to be. When I was photographing the intersection of Broadway and Division Street, I could not get the image of the United States Hotel out of my mind. I was experiencing mixed feelings. It was nice to see the prosperity in Saratoga Springs but I couldn't help thinking that it had lost something.

As I was driving home, I began to understand the words of Thomas Wolfe which kept echoing in my mind: *You Can't Go Home Again.*

APPENDIX

There are some things in Saratoga Springs that have remained substantially unchanged since they were built. They are a tribute to the dedication of the men and women who worked hard to preserve them. Some have found other uses than that for which they were originally intended. Others, like the Aldelphi Hotel still serve the public for the same purpose for which they were originally built, although they have been modernized.

This section presents a few of those beautiful structures and is intended as a tribute to the people who saved them for us. All the photos in this section were taken in 2004 by the author.

These beautiful gate columns frame the entrance to the Katrina Trask Staircase in Congress Park.

Once through the gates, a beautiful view of the park emerges over the granite staircase.

The Yaddo Rose Garden, part of the Spencer Trask estate open to the public attracts thousands of visitors every year. The part of the estate closed to the public is the retreat for artists and writers.

A view of the garden's Pegola and sundial. The garden is maintained by the Yaddo Garden Association whose volunteers are to be commended for doing all the necessary work which keep the gardens so beautiful. To find out more about the association and their work, visit their web page at http://www.yaddo.org/garden/.

THE ADELPHI HOTEL

The Adelphi Hotel was constructed in 1877 and is one of the few surviving hotels from the 19th century that is still operating in the High Victorian style in which it was built. A 90 foot porch, called a piazza extends the full length of the building on the second story. The facade is Italianate design with Victorian fretwork capping the tops of the columns. The restoration kept as much of the original as possible while providing all the conveniences that the modern traveler requires.

To learn more about the hotel, visit their website at http://www.adelphihotel.com/

Photo by the author - 2004

Originally a private home built and owned by George S. Batcheller in 1873, the architects were Nichols and Hacott of Albany, New York. It was almost lost to the wrecking ball but was saved and restored in the 11ᵗʰ hour by it's present owners. Learn more about the Inn by visiting the Batcheller Mansion Inn website at http://www.batchellermansioninn.com/.

THE ITALIAN GARDENS - CONGRESS PARK

Photo by the author - 2004

Greek Tritons emerging from the water is a popular theme in many of Rome's fountains such at the Fountain of Trevi and the three fountains at Piazza Novona. These reproductions are of Belgium marble and done on a smaller scale than the fountains that adorn Rome. Many of the statues in the back gardens have been lost to the ravages of time. Only the pillars (one of which is visible in the background) and the sundial (behind the pillar, not visible in the picture) remain from the complete Italian Gardens. We salute the Saratoga Springs Department of Public Works who take such magnificent care of this Saratoga Springs treasure.

Check with the Saratoga Springs History Museum for more information on the Italian Gardens.

THE SPIRT OF LIFE

Photo by the author - 2004

Another art treasure which was the gift of the Trask family, *The Spirit of Life* was dedicated by Katrina Trask in honor of her husband, Spencer Trask. The statue is by Daniel Chester French who also sculptured the Lincoln Memorial. Once again our thanks go to the Saratoga Springs Department of Public Works for the wonderful care given to the Spirit of Life.

Check with the Saratoga Springs History Museum for more information on the Spirit of Life statue and reflecting pool.

AN INVITATION TO ALL READERS

LET YOUR STORY BECOME A PART OF SARATOGA SPRINGS HISTORY

This book is a perpetual work-in-progress. We invite anyone who would like to make a contribution to it to contact the author via the Saratoga Springs History Museum located in the Casino building in Congress Park. We are interested in any stories you may have about life in Saratoga Springs during the 40's and 50's. We are especially interested in old photographs which would illustrate these stories.

If you think you might have something to contribute, please write up a brief description, with your name, address and telephone number. Mark the envelope, "For Lewis M. Elia," and give or mail it to the staff at the Museum. The story will be evaluated and if we decide to use it, the author will contact you for an interview. Please keep in mind that no compensation for the use of your story or photos will be paid and you will have to sign a release giving full, unrestricted rights to the publisher and author for the use of the materials. We will not consider stories about people who are still living. Photos and stories will give full credit to you and/or your family. As an example of a contributed story, see JERRY THE FRUIT MAN on page 67 of this edition.

Part of the proceeds from the sale of this book will benefit the Saratoga Springs History Museum.

Lewis M. Elia
July 2004

Printed in the United States
By Bookmasters